The Integrity Table
- Cookbook -

©2014 Debbie Portell. All Rights Reserved.
This book and the parts there of may not be produced in any form without permission of the writer

TABLE OF CONTENTS

4-5	**Introduction**
6-8	**Thank you to our Sponsors**
9-21	**Meet Our Sponsors**
22-54	**What Does Integrity Mean to Me?**
55-61	**Condiments**
56	Flavored Coffee Creamer
57	Apple Cider Vinaigrette
58	Strawberry Tarragon Dressing
59	Italian Tomato Sauce
60	Mayonnaise
61	Southern Saucy French Dressing
62	Paleo Italian Salad Dressing
63-82	**Sides, Soups & Salads**
64	Garlic Green Beans
65	Roasted Broccoli with Garlic
66	Squash & Basil Soup
67	Mashed Sweet Potatoes
67	Cranberry Sauce
68	Roasted Beets
69	Roasted Carrots
69	Roasted Brussels Sprouts
70	Deviled Eggs
71	Hearty Healthy Chili
72	Hearty Vegetable Soup
73	Romaine Salad with Fresh Strawberries
74	Cauliflower 'Mashed Potatoes'
75	Meat & Veggie Chowder
76	Chili
77	Roasted Rosemary Sweet Potatoes
78	Christmas Crunch Salad
79	Farmer Girl Meats Sweet Potato Chili
80	Spaghetti Squash
81	Basic Cilantro Cauli-Rice
82	Healthy Chicken Soup
83-103	**Main Dishes**
84	Tuna Steak
85	Meatloaf
86	Steak Kabobs
87	Chicken Veggetti
88	Sweet Garlic Chicken
89	Fajita Chicken
90	Slow Cooked Turkey Breast
91	Roasted Butternut Squash
92	Carribean Tilapia & Green Beans
93	Chicken & Spaghetti Squash
94	Bbq Hamburger & Rice
95	Red Hot Chicken
96	Beef Roast with Apples
97	Avocado Chicken Salad
98	Perfectly Oven Roasted Turkey
99	Pan Seared Tilapia with Veggies
100	Turkey & Tomato Stuffed Mushrooms
101	Dijon Almond Crusted Tilapia
102	Crock Pot Turkey Meatballs
103	Integrity Stuffed Peppers
104-124	**Shakes, Smoothies & Desserts**
105	The Balanced Power Shake
106	Nutty Coconut Butter Bars
107	Pumpkin Pie Pecan Mousse
108	Cindy's Protein Pancakes
119	Dan's Weight Gainer Shake
110	Gluten-Free Pumpkin Pie
111	Peanut Butter Protein Cookies
112	Jeri's Pumpkin Indulgence Smoothie
112	Ken's Strawberry Power Smoothie
113	Jeri's Yogurt Delight
114	Apple Oatmeal
115	Caramel Apple Crisp
116	Zucchini Ice Cream Smoothie
117	Yogurt Parfait
118	Protein Pumpkin Bread
119	Gluten-Free Apple Crisp
120	Clean Microwave Chocolate Cake
121	Brown Rice Flour Cinnamon Crisps
122	No Bake Treats
123	Paleo Pumpkin Pie
124-136	**Team Integrity**
137-139	**Dedications**

Integrity – adherence to moral and ethical principles; soundness of moral character; honesty.

Our company began without a name. It began many years ago when I started personal training as a career. I tried to provide a service in a way that others were not. I left the comfort of the corporate conglomerate and went out on my own. I was successful at doing so because what I did was different from what others were hearing and seeing when they visited their local gym.

Integrity was named from one of my previous employees, who has since left to follow his passion and dream to be a high school wrestling coach. We sat in a group one morning and I said, "Lets pray through what we feel we should name our company. I want it to embody what we stand for as trainers, as a nutritional advisor but more importantly as individuals." "How about just the word integrity Deb?" he asked, "Perfect" I said. We all went home and prayed about it. The next day we were sure it was right for us.

My trainers, at each and every facility, are my family. I don't have children of my own, but I've taken on each of these individuals as if they were my own. My own sister or brother. When I hire trainers, I don't look in the newspaper or on the internet. I trust in the Lord and know He will send the next person I need my way. I sincerely stand in faith with each new person and believe that God will bring me someone that believes the way I do. Someone that has the same passion in their heart towards healing and wellness. Most of my trainers, at one point in time, were clients of mine. All of my trainers have a story to tell. Some have lost 100lbs. Some have battled disease. Some still battle. All of them encompass the definition of Integrity. They live their trade. They not only practice what they preach, they live it.

"Train to Live" is my motto for our company; Our creed I guess you could say. It means what it says. Train to be able to live the best life possible. Don't live to train. Don't get so involved in it that it consumes you and ultimately becomes unhealthy because you are willing to go to any degree to look better. Train because you want to feel good first and looking good will always follow. Eat to live. Food is ultimately the fuel that will determine the path of which you will follow on a daily basis. It will either be a path to freedom and health or a path to sickness and disease.

You could say I LIVE TO TRAIN. To train others that is. I live my life as a servant to the Lord. I adhere to what he wants for me or I sure try. I feel the call God has placed on my life is to serve others to the best of my ability to achieve optimal health through nutrition and exercise. I believe diseases can be healed by simply making different food choices. I can say this because I have done it with my own body. In my first book, **Clean Eating, Clean Thinking, Clean Living,** I go into great detail about the health issues I have dealt with over the years and how food healed my body. I have also spent 10 years working with individuals helping them to do exactly that. It is remarkable to witness as Type II diabetes or high blood pressure gets wiped out in 2 weeks by simply changing an individual's food.

Over the years, my clients have also become my family, even though I don't speak much about my personal life with them. In fact, most of them know very little about me personally, other than what you can read in my book. However, they can see my heart and know it is pure and sincere. They see that my end result everyday is to help them achieve their dreams in the healthiest and most effective way possible. I have witnessed wonderful relationships being built during my group training sessions. They have sincerely become a family. They do early morning cardio together. They share recipes. They travel with each other to give support. They honestly take stock in each other's success and work towards truly helping each other stay focused and succeed.

It is amazing to watch. To know that I have anything to do with such a fantastic group of individuals is humbling. I praise God daily for the life He has given me and the opportunities He has set before me. To Him be all the Glory because without Him I would have nothing and do nothing.

Simply because it is clean eating, doesn't mean it can't taste good. Don't make excuses for bad choices. You either choose health or you choose disease for you body. Don't use a holiday as a reason to take yourself down a road you know you don't want to travel. Every bad decision leaves a lasting impact on your health and your body. Make each decision count. If you go the wrong direction, correct it. Every new meal is a new chance at feeling great. Just get right back on track. Don't look back. Don't ride the road of defeat. Life is too short for that. Mistakes happen and we've all fallen short. Just make the decision to get back on the right road. Clean eating, clean thinking and clean living. All three will lead you down a road of health, wellness and happiness.

God Bless you on your journey.

Debbie Portell

TRAIN TO LIVE

Many Thanks to our Sponsors.

Powerhouse Gym

I have worked for Powerhouse Gym going on 10 years now and have loved every minute of it.
Powerhouse is home to me and always will be. There is nothing else like it in St. Louis. It features 30,000 square feet of pure gym; No pool and no basketball court. And what's more, we have a 9,000 square foot Cross Fit Facility! But probably the most unique quality of the Powerhouse, is in its ability to attract such a wide range of people. I watch as individuals from those in their 70's, to clients trying to drop 100lbs, to professional athletes, to just the typical person trying to stay healthy, all in one location trying to make a change for the better. I truly feel like Powerhouse is more than a gym; it is a healing center. You can't leave the place without feeling better. It has history and I know that each and every one of my clients would agree when I say that we are fortunate to be a part of it. But before my journey at Powerhouse began, I met Roger Semsch, founder of the St. Louis Power House Gym. At first, Roger managed my nutrition as I prepped for my figure competitions. However, once I witnessed the amazing impact he had on my health, I knew I wanted to continue to work with him, even after I stopped competing. Roger Semsch has dedicated his life to his employees, members and clients. God bless his heart and dedication to the fitness industry. I am blessed to know and work so closely with him.

Complete Fitness

I'm excited to say we will be celebrating our 2 year anniversary in March of 2015 and will be adding Cross Fit this year as well! This is a beautiful fitness center with such an amazing team of trainers and employees. They genuinely feel like a second family to me. Nothing about the work I do at Complete feels like "just a job". The members here are real people, all working hard with a goal to stay healthy; each one is fighting their own battle of heart disease, diabetes, arthritis and/or injury recovery. This is not a corporate conglomerate. It's owned and managed by Todd and Dan, two wonderful people that I feel blessed to work for. They care deeply about the health and wellness of their members. They continually surprise me with the kindness, generosity and consideration they show to their members and employees.

Ladue PT

I feel fortunate to have the opportunity to work with Joe Olivastro. He has worked as a successful personal trainer and business owner for 24 years. Accomplishments such as these are rare in the fitness industry, to say the least. His facility has a distinct, boutique type ambiance that leaves you with a soothing Zen feeling. I love working out of this location. The staff is warm and inviting. The location itself is nestled into a quaint shopping community in the heart of the Ladue marketplace. Joe is well known for his group and private Yoga instruction. Our Integrity team of trainers are impacting and changing lives daily from Ladue PT. We offer Physical Therapy with Kyle Weindel, as well my own services of Integrity Personal Training and Nutrition. We also have Jay Robb, Barleans and Now Foods brand supplements just as our other two facilities do.

Energy Therapies and Massage

I first met with Elaine after having a very serious concussion. I started wearing glasses after the injury because my vision went blurry. I was dizzy all day, every day. She performed cranial therapy on me twice a week for 6 months. Along with the help of my chiropractor, Elaine made it possible for me to see clearly again. I still continued to work as a trainer but had not worked out for over 9 months. My entire body had seized up after the injury. She not only had to work to realign some of the bones in my cranium but she then had to work at releasing all of my muscles from head to toe. After releasing my muscles and working

Many Thanks to our Sponsors.

through the trigger points, my lymph system was in over drive. I was swelling in places I had never swelled before. Elaine did a wonderful job of draining my lymph system, which reduced the swelling and, eventually, that led to the release of necessary toxins from my system. I don't think of Elaine as a massage therapist. I think of her as a healer. She is a remarkable woman who I know God sent to me. I don't know where I'd be today without her.

Dr. Ian McDonald, Chiropractor

I also began seeing Dr. Ian after working with Elaine. Ian does a slightly different style of Chiropractic Medicine than any other Chiropractor I had been to over the years. The technique he uses is known as Active Release Therapy, or A.R.T. for short. I send a large portion of my client base to Dr. McDonald. I believe without preparing the soft tissue first, your body will not be able to hold an adjustment. Ian first finds the areas where scar tissue has built up, then works through those trigger points to release them and finishes with the adjustment. It makes all the difference in the world to have this work done prior to the adjustment. I have noticed significant changes in my physique and my clients' bodies just from working with Ian consistently. His work not only changes the way they feel but also the way they look. The results stick with the client. I would recommend everyone work with a Chiropractor like Ian at least one time a month to keep everything in alignment.

Missouri Onsite Massage

I work with Dawn on detailed thorough sports style massage. She has experience in working with all types of individual massage needs. She works with my clients that have very specific issues. Especially forward shoulder rotation. She does a wonderful job of releasing the pecs, traps, delts and lats. I have worked with several massage therapists over the years and none of them released my delts or pecs. I just continued to stay tight in that area. I feel the primary areas for release are traps, SCM or neck, delts, pecs, lats, hips and IT Band. I feel Dawn does this in a way that I have not ever had done before. She has an in home service which I have used and found it so helpful to not have to leave my home. She also has a very relaxing location in Lake St. Louis. I have several clients that use Dawn for massage and have achieved a great deal of relief from her work.

Dr. Richard Bligh

Dr. Bligh is my primary care physician. I have worked with him for 6 years now. He has helped me to regulate my thyroid in a way that no other Dr. was able to. He has also helped me to gain control of my out of control Estrogen levels. My negative Estrogen was through the roof when I first met him. Every visit I have with him he spends a minimum of 30 minutes with me. His staff is friendly and always goes out of their way to assist me with anything I need. I have sent several of my clients to Dr. Bligh and he has been able to finally get to the bottom of what several doctors have missed or skirted around for years. His office does Hormone Replacement Therapy as well. I would highly recommend considering Dr. Bligh as a primary care physician or if you are considering Hormone Replacement Therapy.

Farmer Girl Meats

I can't say enough great things about this company. The meat is exceptional and it is delivered directly to your door. The taste of these meats are so good, that I find myself not wanting to eat meat unless I know it came directly from The Farmer Girl or a similar place. I can honestly say that I taste the difference between Farmer Girl Meats and store bought meat. If you compared a

Many Thanks to our Sponsors.

chicken breast sold at a local grocery store and one from Farmer Girl Meats, the difference is actually frightening. The chicken today is being pumped with extreme amounts of estrogen builders. This excess estrogen is the leading cause of breast, cervical and uterine cancer today and is the reason my negative estrogen is through the roof. My levels went down by 60 points within 3 months just from changing to organic, hormone free, farm fresh, grass fed meats and dairy. Another remarkable difference is in the beef. I can brown 5 lbs of beef from Farmer Girl and I will genuinely feel no need to drain the meat. I always do, but I truly do not have much to drain off of it. As for the typical beef I get from the grocery store, I actually have to drain midway and at the end of cooking. Give Farmer Girl Meats a try. I guarantee you will not only taste the difference but you will notice a difference in the way you feel.

The Coconut Kitchen
This is a wonderful company that has created such a unique product. She has taken a healthy fat source in coconut oil and combined clean eating additives to make it flavorful and useful as a snack. I have always recommended liquid MCT oil as a use for fatty acids in a meal. Medium Chain Triglycerides are broken down and used as energy much differently than typical fats. I find that my clients see increased strength and energy levels when using MCT oil, as well as improvement in overall tone of the muscle. Another benefit to MCT oil, are the thermogenic properties it possesses. I love the coconut butter that I receive from The Coconut Kitchen. I also feel good knowing she uses only natural ingredients such as raw nuts, lemon, stevia, cocoa powder and cinnamon to flavor it. I would suggest 1 tablespoon of her coconut butter as a snack daily in between meals to keep you satiated until your next meal. Soon, you will be able to find this product at all 3 of our facilities.

The White Hare
The first time I walked into this place I sent John a text stating, "Don't come for me. I have died and gone to heaven." This store is absolutely gorgeous. I have purchased all of my holiday decorations and regular home decorations from The White Hare. They have made several custom arrangements and wreaths as well as assisted me with all of the decorations for my Christmas trees. I can't say enough great things about this store. I used to drive into Wildwood or Clayton for all of my decorating needs and now I don't even drive over the river. I always look forward to a monthly escape into this store on my day off. They have reasonable prices and one of a kind furniture and products. When I post pictures of my home, you can be sure I purchased them from The White Hare. I would highly recommend you visit the shop. I know you won't leave empty handed!

Trail Smokehouse
This is a quaint destination restaurant located right off the Katy trail. It is a great place to visit when you are out for a bike ride, but definitely worth the drive as well if you aren't. Our selections for clean eating in the area are minimal. Not only does it provide delicious Integrity approved meals, but it also has a wonderful atmosphere and beautiful surroundings. The drive is short but enjoyable. My client Kelly Brazil has worked hard at cleaning up her lifestyle and has made significant changes in her health because of it. I couldn't be more proud of her efforts. Her personal training with Mike and nutrition counseling with myself has caused her to have a contagious spirit, which allows us to have a wonderful place to enjoy a great tasting and clean meal! This is a necessary destination for you for lunch or dinner this spring.

Our Sponsors

POWERHOUSE GYM®
St. Louis

77 Kenrick Plaza • St. Louis, MO
(314) 968-3113

Open 24 Hours - 30,000 Sq ft Facility
Juice Bar (protein Shake/Health Shake) - Child Care Available
Supplement Store Onsite - Top Notch Personal Trainers
Now Offering CrossFit!

Complete FITNESS

Open **24 hours**
Kids **Play**
Free **Classes**
No **Contracts**

6225 Ronald Reagan Drive • Lake St. Louis, MO 63367 • [636] 614.1180

Find us on Facebook: //www.facebook.com/CompleteFitnessLsl

www.completefitnesslsl.com

ladue PT
Personal Training · Nutrition · Physical Therapy

9751 Clayton Rd • Ladue MO 63124
(314) 432-BODY

www.laduept.com

Center for Energy Therapies & Massage
with Elaine Lankford

Deep Muscle Massage • Reflexology (Zone Therapy) • Shiatsu & Accupressure
Sports Massage • Swedish Massage • Trigger Point Therapy (a.k.a.)
Myotherapy or Neuromuscular Therapy • Myo-Fascial Release • Nett

(314) 704-3664
520 Huber Park Court
Weldon Spring, MO 63304

Email: elainelankford@gmail.com
Website: mpmt.patientcal.com/

Ian McDonald DC

936 Chesterfield Parkway East
Chesterfield, MO 63017
Phone: 636-537-0564
Web: www.CMBchiro.com
Email: Ian.McDonaldDC@gmail.com

Missouri Onsite Massage

Dawn Von Burg-Keller
massageonsite@centurytel.net
920 Bent Oat Ct. Suite E
Lake St. Louis, MO
636.795.1823
lic#2001012596

Swedish Massage, Prenatal Massage, Deep Tissue Massage, Fijian Barefoot Massage, Acupressure Facelift, Hot Stone Massage, Sole Rejuvenator, Sinus Relief, Aromatherapy Body Wrap, Ear Candling, Paraffin Therapy

Dr. Bligh

Concierge Medicine

Concierge medicine, also known as retainer medicine and boutique medicine, enables our patients to receive highly personalized healthcare in a comfortable, relaxed setting for an annual retainer fee. In combination with our wide array of age management and cosmextic services, our patients receive comprehensive, holistic, individualized healthcare.

Hormone Replacement

Dr. Bligh utilizes bio-identical hormone replacement therapy. The hormone replacement pellets are superior to synthetic hormone replacement options because the bio-identical hormones are metabolized by the body. Bio-identical hormone therapy can reduce common menopause or andropause symptoms and improves your overall physical well-being and quality of life.

Cosmetic Services

Dr. Bligh and his esthetician offer a wide variety of procedures, ranging from neurotoxin injection (aka botox or xeomin) to laser lipolysis. Consultations are offered at no charge, so schedule yours today to see which treatment options are the best fit for your needs.

SCHEDULE AN APPOINTMENT
TODAY!

777 South New Ballas Rd, Suite 200E, St. Louis, MO 63141 | **314.994.1536** | www.drblighmd.com

Farmer Girl Meats

Clean, healthy, straight-from-the-farm meats.

GRASSFED BEEF   PASTURED RAISED   PASTURE RAISED PORK   PASTURE RAISED LAMB

Delivered to your doorstep.

Take a gander at our farm-fresh meat selection at our online store
www.farmergirlmeats.com!

Warrenton, Missouri   www.farmergirlmeats.com   Order Online Today!

What Does Integrity Mean to Me?

What Does Integrity Mean to Me?

" Integrity is doing the right thing when no one is around. "The true test of a mans character is what he does when no one is watching."

Debbie Portell & Adam Coffey

Adam Coffey
Personal Trainer for Integrity Training Systems at Powerhouse Gym St. Louis & Ladue PT

Aimee & Debbie
2014

What Does Integrity Mean to Me?

"Integrity to me means strong; strong in your desire to achieve your goals, strong work ethic, strength in believing in yourself and helping others achieve their best. This is what Debbie's Integrity Training provides for all of us and expects of us. No matter your health issues, setbacks, age, or obstacles; you can succeed."

Aimee Nassif
Personal Training Client of Debbie Portell
at Powerhouse Gym StL and Complete Fitness

The Carl Family 2014

What Does Integrity Mean to Me?

"Integrity is doing the right thing, keeping promises, being authentic – especially when it's most difficult. Its rewards are significant and increase exponentially as situations become more challenging. It has the power to build bridges between unsuspecting people and bestow the gift of gratitude on those who choose it. Life is better when lived with integrity!"

Angie Carl
Owner of My Coconut Kitchen

Ben Lueken & Caity Hawksley
2014

What Does Integrity Mean to Me?

"The strength of Integrity is found within the name. We are true to our word. We are a team of dedicated professionals with a passion for the science of human movement. Our message isn't clouded with commercial gimmicks. What we do promise you is our time, our passion, and our knowledge. That is the foundation of Integrity. Changing people's lives one rep, one set at a time."

Ben Lueken
Personal Trainer for Integrity Training Systems at Powerhouse Gym St. Louis & Ladue PT

Mike, Debbie & Beverly
2014

What Does Integrity Mean to Me?

" My wife and I have been training & following a Nutrition program from Debbie Portell with Integrity Training Systems for the last several months. Not only have we experienced great strides in reaching our goals physically, but have also seen a big difference in how we feel. We've both experienced higher energy levels and we even sleep better. We have been working out for the majority of our life but we both agree, without a doubt, that the expertise and personal attention to our personal goals are second to none."

Mike & Beverly Sloan
Personal Training Clients of Debbie Portell at Complete Fitness

What Does Integrity Mean to Me?

Brad Cadwallader & Debbie Portell 2014

"Integrity to me means "family". Not just showing up and working out for an hour together. But spending time with friends and living a healthier life. Integrity means when it is a rainy and cold Tuesday night, and you don't want to leave your house and want to just lay on the couch and watch TV, there is a "family" that is waiting and wanting you to show up and complete that workout. It doesn't just help you become a better person, but allows you to help motivate others in your "family" to become better and healthier. Joining Integrity showed me that I was not alone in my fight to become healthy. I found that there were other people just like me struggling with the in-and-outs of trying to lose weight. It does not matter if you have been working out for 10 years or 10 minutes, this "family" accepts you and pushes you beyond what you thought was possible and makes you believe in yourself.

Debbie and Integrity not only provide you with your workout for the day or week, but make sure your are good the rest of the off time as well. She goes above and beyond what a personal trainer is and should be. She has pushed me to be the best that I have ever been, in my workouts and in my everyday life. She believes in you like "FAMILY".

Brad Cadwallader
Personal Training Client of Debbie Portell
at Complete Fitness and Powerhouse Gym Stl

Cecilia & Cory Gray
2014

What Does Integrity Mean to Me?

" To me, Integrity means staying the 2nd hour at the gym even though I want to call it quits. It means working out harder than any of my friends and staying in shape through my long pregnancy. Being around positive, enthusiastic people while working out in a group is irreplaceable- it is hard to go back to working out on my own now! "

Cecilia Gray
Personal Training Client of Debbie Portell at Powerhouse Gym Stl

Cindy Mantia
2014

What Does Integrity Mean to Me?

"As I look back on almost a decade of "Lifestyle Change," I realize that a journey always begins with one single step. That step happened in 2007 after reaching my heaviest weight of 196 lbs. I walked into Powerhouse Gym and met Debbie Portell. I decided to start a workout and nutrition program. As my personal trainer for 8 years. Debbie has helped me achieve goals that I thought were unattainable. Debbie encouraged me to do my first Figure and Bodybuilding Show in 2009. That night was unbelievable I won 1st in Master Figure and received my IFPA pro-card. I also took 1st in Masters Bodybuilding and 2nd in Novice Bodybuilding. Even after this tremendous accomplishment I will never forget where this journey started and that was with Debbie. Her knowledge of training, clean eating, and trying new techniques is why I continue to see results. I am a firm believer in Debbie Portell and that is why I embody a healthy lifestyle.

So take that first step you won't regret it."

Cindy Mantia
Personal Training Client of Debbie Portell
at Powerhouse Gym Stl

What Does Integrity Mean to Me?

" It means healthier living through better nutrition and fitness. "

Debbie Portell & Dan Hoormann
2014

Dan Hoormann
Owner of Complete Fitness

Dave & Debbie 2014

What Does Integrity Mean to Me?

INTEGRITY represents not just doing things right, but always doing the right things.

Integrity Training Systems is a true example of that. Through real, true and healthy nutritional guidance, Team Integrity is changing lives every day and will continue to change lives for years to come, always living by the very simple, but important, motto: "Train to Live."

Dave DeRemer
Dfac Pro Men's Physique Competitor
Team Integrity Client

What Does Integrity Mean to Me?

"The characteristics of an individual with integrity is very similar to those of a diamond. Rare, strong, transparent, valuable and although they may have flaws, they don't define them. These "flaws" make each and every one unique and beautiful."

Debbie & Dee Dee
2014

Dee Dee Fetouh
Personal Training Client of Debbie Portell at Complete Fitness

What Does Integrity Mean to Me?

"Integrity to me means truthful dependability. Always knowing I am going to get the best of what or who a person is."

Debbie & Elaine 2014

Elaine Lankford
Massage Therapist, Owner of Energy Therapies & Massage

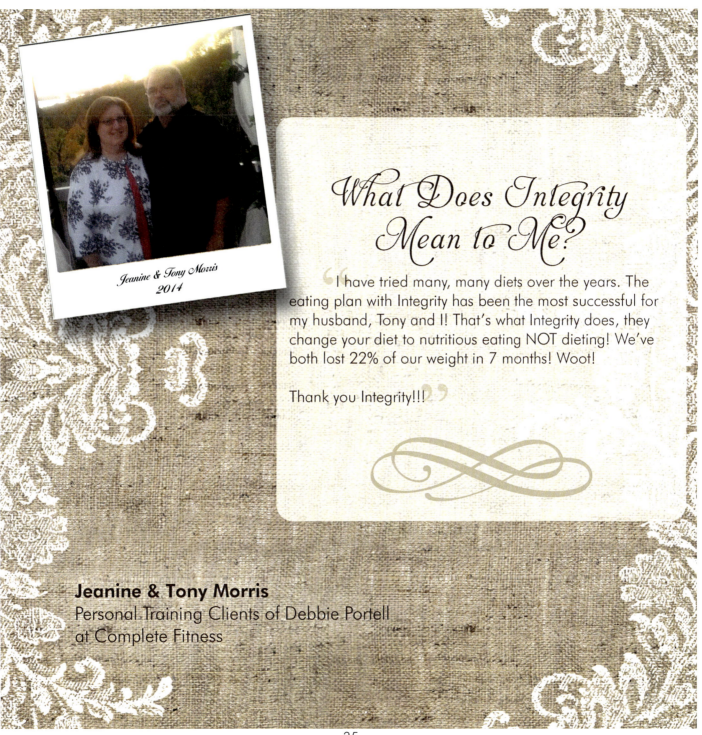

Jeanine & Tony Morris
2014

What Does Integrity Mean to Me?

"I have tried many, many diets over the years. The eating plan with Integrity has been the most successful for my husband, Tony and I! That's what Integrity does, they change your diet to nutritious eating NOT dieting! We've both lost 22% of our weight in 7 months! Woot!

Thank you Integrity!!!"

Jeanine & Tony Morris
Personal Training Clients of Debbie Portell at Complete Fitness

What Does Integrity Mean to Me?

Debbie and Jeri

Mike Harris & Jeri Madison

Jeri Madison
Integrity Training Systems Client at Complete Fitness, Nutrition with Debbie, Training with Mike

" If you look up the meaning of "Integrity", you find it refers to the qualities of honesty and fairness, as well as the state of being complete. Debbie Portell has built her company on those qualities.

I have been into fitness and healthy eating since my teens, but I always found the information out there to be overwhelming and often conflicting. I thought I was doing the right things, but ended up with injuries and a few extra pounds. In early 2013, I finally found someone who cared about treating the "complete" person. Debbie customized my nutrition for optimal health, paired me with the right trainer for my fitness goals, helped me to stay focused on success, and referred me to great practitioners to address other health challenges.

The story doesn't stop there…Debbie and her staff are like family to me. She continues to check in on how I'm doing with my fitness goals and we tweak my diet when needed. I train with one of her trainers several days a week. And, some of the best benefits have been watching my husband's progress when he decided to see Debbie for nutrition and that of several friends who are also changing their lives for the better with Integrity. "

Jessica & Debbie
2014

What Does Integrity Mean to Me?

"Being part of the Integrity team has encouraged me to push myself in ways that I didn't think was possible. While training with Integrity, I have gained a new confidence and motivation to be and do better. Not just with my diet and workouts, but in my everyday life. Integrity has improved my life, as well as the life of my family. The Integrity team has pushed me when I wanted to give up or didn't think I was capable. The men and women of this team are more than just a team it is truly a family. We all care about each other's goals and are there to root for them and drag them to the finish line. I am proud to say that I have not only gained a team, but I have gained many life long friendships with Integrity."

Jessica Revere
Personal Training Client of Debbie Portell
at Powerhouse Gym Stl & Complete Fitness

What Does Integrity Mean to Me?

"Partnering with Integrity has provided the opportunity to work with a team of individuals who are voracious about their ability to deliver results. Integrity is a culture of well-being that presents nutrition and fitness in a straight forward, professional and honorable manner. Integrity ignites the fire that brings on results!"

John, Debbie & Joe
2014

Joe Olivastro
Owner of Ladue PT

John Morris (Before)

John Morris (After)

John Morris
Personal Trainer for Integrity Training Systems at Complete Fitness and Ladue PT

What Does Integrity Mean to Me?

"When I first began with Integrity Training Systems I was physically, mentally, and spiritually broken. I was a career Police Officer who had become overweight to the point of having heart issues at a very young age. When I decided I needed help, I was referred to Debbie Portell by a friend. I began Debbie's nutrition program and started training with her twice a week. I was not only able to lose weight, but I also became mentally and spiritually stronger as well.

The clean food I consumed fueled my brain in a way I had never been fueled before. I found myself thinking clearer and feeling better. Not only was my health improving but so was my attitude. People began to ask me what I was doing because my body had began to change dramatically. I had not even realized how much weight I lost because I was so focused on how fantastic I felt. Debbie helped me lose 68 pounds! My weight dropped from 286 to 218 just from proper training and nutrition! Then, I decided I wanted to gain some muscle and she helped me gain 38 pounds going from 218 to 256. Again, this was all done by properly changing my nutrition and training.

After witnessing the radical change in my mind, body, and spirit I knew I had to help other people do this for a living. I left the only career I knew to pursue a life as a personal trainer for Integrity Training Systems. I praise God for the opportunity and am thankful every day to be where I am.

Remember, you do not have to feel great to start. But you do have to start to feel great. Don't wait for tomorrow."

What Does Integrity Mean to Me?

"What Integrity Training is to me ... Sincere smiles whenever I walk in the door; non-judgemental, yet bold direction without accepting excuses; an appreciation of effort; words of encouragement to just keep moving forward.

The definitions of the concepts "train to live" and "feel good, look good", have unique meanings to each individual. Everyone has a story. Getting to one's ideal is a personal journey. Like any journey, moving from point A to point B will have varying degrees of successes and setbacks.

The time to reach ones destination is also unique. For some it may be a quick sprint, for others a marathon. Regardless, it requires an inner desire greater than the perceived mental or physical cost.

Regardless of whether your journey is a sprint or a marathon; and your vision is to simply be healthy or a professional competitor ... You can rest assured the Integrity trainers will meet you where you are every day, and then walk alongside you on your journey. You will receive customized training and nutrition coaching unique to your lifestyle, life cycle, and physical health. What the trainers cannot provide personally, they will offer outsourcing services for your consideration.

All along my journey, the Integrity Training team continues to provide enthusiastic support, encouragement to pull from inner strength, and a daily celebration of progress. Debbie, John, Lisa, Sandy and Mike have walked alongside me, cheering me to a daily victory. What I've come to appreciate about this team is that each trainer has walked the same road, experienced the same emotional and physical challenges and are living examples of Debbie's philosophies about achieving and living the healthiest one is capable of being: physically, emotionally and spiritually.

My two mantras are: "If you can conceive it; you can achieve it!" and "Act as if <blank>."(you fill in the blank.)

Best wishes for finishing YOUR journey,"

Karen Schneider

Karen Schneider
Personal Training Client of Debbie Portell at Complete Fitness

Kim & Debbie
2014

What Does Integrity Mean to Me?

"I have been training with Debbie Portell and Integrity Training for 2 years. She has helped me prep for several shows and I have learned so much from her about nutrition and workouts. I would not be where I am today in my fitness journey without her in my life. It has also been so wonderful to be a part of a team like Integrity, everyone is so encouraging and supportive of each other. Deb's passion and love for helping other people shows in everything she does. She is amazing."

Kim Lipe
Personal Training Client of Debbie Portell
at Powerhouse Gym Stl

Jerome & Kim Simon Family
2014

What Does Integrity Mean to Me?

"To me, Integrity means…….the love and support I get from being part of a larger family/team. Debbie not only provides not only the structure and program, but a group of individuals committed to looking and feeling better with clean eating. And we don't just sweat together in the gym, but we also share stories and struggles that keep us motivated. You are NEVER alone :). Placing myself as a priority has helped me improve the quality of time I spend with my family. I have also set a good example for my teenage daughters so they know how to eat and why it is so important. On Sunday afternoons when the weather is nice, you will find my family relaxing under a park tree listening to Debbie's talk show after enjoying an Integrity picnic lunch and long walk with the dogs.

Kimberly Simon
Personal Training Client of Debbie Portell at Complete Fitness

Lisa, Elaine, Sandy & Debbie
2014

What Does Integrity Mean to Me?

" To me, integrity means living the life you are meant to, regardless of outside influences....deciding what your values, priorities and beliefs are, then living an unwavering life that supports them. It means finding what pushes you to be the best that you can be, and living it day in and day out. I could not be more proud to be a part of Integrity Training group because I feel like that is exactly what we do. We push each other to be the best versions of ourselves, and allow our clients to do the same. "

Lisa Klaus
Personal Trainer for Integrity Training Systems at Complete Fitness & Ladue PT

Maribel Hernandez & Charles William Hedge
2014

What Does Integrity Mean to Me?

"Integrity means family. Integrity has the power to change your life, with love, caring and encouragement. It's a circle of trust."

Maribel Hernandez
Personal Training Client of Debbie Portell at Powerhouse Gym Stl & Complete Fitness

Misti, Debbie, Dee Dee & Megan
2014

What Does Integrity Mean to Me?

"Being a part of Integrity has been like having a second family. Great co-workers, teamwork, and lifting each other up to be the best we can be. Whether in training, shows, or life itself, we have each others back. If we have questions, or want to bounce ideas off of each other, need motivation, or new ideas; I feel comfortable knowing that we can count on each other for assistance in any area. Being a part of Integrity has made me love going to work, love my job and really appreciate the similarities AND differences that make us …. Well,… Integrity. :)"

Megan Kenkel
Personal Trainer for Integrity Training Systems
at Complete Fitness

Melissa, Sandy & Megan
2014

What Does Integrity Mean to Me?

" Life is a journey, not a race, and Integrity Training is what you need next to you for the ride. They push you to go further than you ever thought you could. They help and encourage you when it gets tough and you want to take the easier route of just giving up. They celebrate your successes and amazing progress. When you fall, they will pick you up, help dust you off and get you back on track without fault or condescendence because they've all been there at some state of their journey. Eventually you begin to change your thinking instead of "They", it becomes "We". We are a TEAM. If you join the team you will find strength you never knew you had. You can do this, you deserve this because at Integrity you belong! "

Melissa Lafferty
Personal Training Client of Debbie Portell
at Complete Fitness

What Does Integrity Mean to Me?

"Integrity to me, is more than my career and the company I work for; It is a family. A combination of like minded individuals who share a common goal and passion for fitness, health, and everything that goes along with it. I know I am very fortunate to be able to do something that I love everyday and it is because of Integrity Training Systems that I am able to do so."

Mike Harris & Debbie

Mike Harris
Personal Trainer for Integrity Training Systems at Complete Fitness

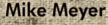

Mike Meyer & Debbie
2014

What Does Integrity Mean to Me?

"INTEGRITY = FAMILY
The Integrity team has been nothing but supportive, never judgmental, and fully accepting of me as I am, all my faults, flaws, and shortcomings included. I have thrived under their support, guidance, and friendship not only growing in my knowledge of living a healthier lifestyle, but becoming more confident in myself as a person. I no longer walk with my head held low staring at the ground, but held high safe in the knowledge my Integrity team, my extended family, is in my corner for all aspects of my life. They are there to celebrate my successes or to offer a shoulder to cry on when needed. They offer me unconditional love and support just like a family. This is why to me...... INTEGRITY IS FAMILY! !!"

Mike Meyer
Personal Training Client of Debbie Portell
at Complete Fitness

What Does Integrity Mean to Me?

Misti & Debbie 2014

Misti Weatherford
Personal Training Client of Debbie Portell at Complete Fitness & Powerhouse Gym Stl

" It has been an absolute privilege to be a part of Team Integrity. Few people ever get the opportunity to experience the support of amazing people who lift and elevate the performance of an individual to heights never before achieved. Within Team Integrity, you find the motivation, inspiration, knowledge and all the support needed to reach goals you've only dreamed of. For myself, I have completely transformed -- not only physically, but emotionally as well. The strength I have gained in such a short amount of time is amazing, but the passion I have discovered for this industry, and the people within it, is indescribable. Each member of Team Integrity has brought so much joy to my life. Though we may all have different goals, we still support and motivate each other to be the best we can be. When you find people who encourage you to become a better you every day, you discover that together you can achieve anything! The key factor to the success of Team Integrity lies within little, fierce Debbie Portell -- the glue that keep us all together. She has this incredible ability to push you toward your fitness goals in a way that forever becomes your lifestyle. Team Integrity truly is a way to "Train to Live," and THAT, is absolutely priceless. "

"Team Integrity is always a team, but FOREVER a family!"

Debbie & Monica

What Does Integrity Mean to Me?

" In life, I have learned in order to be the best you must be willing to give your all. I find that working with Integrity, I am pushed beyond limits which forces me to grow stronger and achieve positive results. I find it very rewarding to be able to have both personal training and nutritional services provided through the same health vehicle – Integrity Training Systems (ITS). By training with Integrity and utilizing the nutritional sessions, the trainer is able to monitor my progress on a weekly basic and tweak the workout program or modify nutritional plan as needed. Training with Integrity feels like a second family where everyone is encouraging and cheering you to the finished line. "

Monica Thornton
Personal Training Client of Debbie Portell
at Powerhouse Gym Stl & Complete Fitness

Natasha, Ella, Connor, Debbie & Sophia
2014

What Does Integrity Mean to Me?

"Integrity to me is more than a word, it's a family. Everyone in the Integrity family is loving, kind, heartwarming and just a wonderful group of people feeding off of Debbie's sunshine. It's amazing to be apart of! You can see it in all the relationships that every person of Integrity has with their clients, teammates, peers and coworkers. You really can't tell who's been a friend for a day, or a lifelong friend for years. That's the bond we all share being apart of the Integrity family, I am so thankful and blessed to be a part of it!"

Natasha Summers
Assistant to Debbie Portell

Roger & Debbie

What Does Integrity Mean to Me?

integrity
[in-teg-ri-tee]

1. adherence to moral and ethical principles; soundness of moral character; honesty.

Twenty-six years ago I started in the fitness business. I quickly found out there were very little ethical principles soon after I began my first fitness center. Since then, I have found others that share my passion for sound moral character. Now, I work with others here at Integrity training and have found even more people wanting to share my honesty in giving our clients the most in fitness education and instruction.

Roger Semsch
Owner of Powerhouse Gym St. Louis

Misti, Debbie & Sandy

What Does Integrity Mean to Me?

"What Integrity means to me is Family. A group of wonderful people who have come to be my support who share in the same passion I do. Caring friends I can look to for love and support when I need it and the push and drive I need to get to the next level. Integrity and Debbie Portell have a very special place in my heart. I love being a part of Integrity, representing a team and woman who stands for what she truly believes in heart and soul."

Sandra Singer
Personal Trainer for Integrity Training Systems at Complete Fitness and Personal Training Client of Debbie Portell

Dee Dee & Wilma
2014

What Does Integrity Mean to Me?

"Integrity training is an important part of my life! Integrity offers a wealth of information! Ranging from topics on exercise techniques and programming to a healthy lifestyle choices! The Personal trainers from Integrity are motivated, accountable and go the extra mile to achieve your fitness goals! I am very fortunate to be able to work with Debbie Portell and all the trainers from Integrity! Its a dream come true! Thank you Debbie and all Integrity trainers for all your hard work!"

Wilma Weinkein
Front Desk Staff, Complete Fitness
Personal Training Client of Debbie Portell

Flavored Coffee Creamer

1 cup Unsweetened Vanilla Almond Milk
1 (12oz can) Fat Free Evaporated Milk
1 tbsp Stevia in the Raw
Pinch of Salt
2 tsp Alcohol Free Vanilla Extract

Mix together all ingredients and add to your favorite coffee.

Sophia & Debbie
2014

Apple Cider Vinaigrette

Fremont Dorsey & Debbie
2014

1/4 cup Apple Cider Vinegar
1 Garlic clove, minced
1/2 tsp Onion Powder
1/2 tbsp Stevia in the Raw
1 tsp Spicy Brown Mustard
1/3 cup of Olive Oil

Whisk together first 4 ingredients, add oil in a slow steady stream, whisking constantly until smooth. Add salt and pepper to taste. Makes about 2/3 cup.

Strawberry Tarragon Dressing

4 cups of Strawberries, hulled & sliced
1 medium Shallot, minced
1/2 cup Balsamic Vinegar
1/2 tsp freshly ground White Pepper
1/2 cup Agave Nectar or brown rice syrup
1 tbsp Dried Tarragon
1 tsp Salt

Puree all the dressing ingredients in a blender until smooth and creamy, stopping once or twice to scrape down the sides. Toss Strawberry Tarragon Dressing to taste with Elaine's Romaine Salad with Fresh Strawberries recipe on page 73.

Elaine Lankford 2014

Italian Tomato Sauce

2 large cans Tomato Sauce
1 large can Chopped Tomatoes
1 small Onion sauteed
2 cloves Garlic, minced and sauteed
1 tbsp Italian Seasoning
1 tbsp Oregano
1 tbsp Onion Powder
1/2 tsp Red Pepper flakes
2-3 tbsp Stevia in the Raw
3 dash of Franks Hot Sauce
1/2 tbsp Black Pepper
2 tsp Salt

Saute veggies. Combine all ingredients, slow simmer for 20 minutes.

Kim & Ken Stogsdill
2014

Kim & Debbie
2014

Mayonnaise

2 large yolks
1 tsp Dijon Mustard
4 tsp Lemon Juice
1 cup Olive Oil
1 tsp Stevia
2 dashes Tabasco
Salt & Pepper to taste

Place all ingredients, except oil, in blender. Mix well. Add oil slowly until emulsified. Salt and pepper to taste. Use pasteurized organic eggs to avoid using raw eggs. Keep stored in fridge for 1 week.

Debbie Portell

Roasted Pepper Mayo

2 large yolks
1 jar Roasted Red Pepper, pat dry
1 Garlic clove minced
1 tsp Dijon Mustard
4 tsp Lemon Juice
1 cup Olive Oil
1 tsp Stevia in the Raw
1 dash Tabasco
Salt & Pepper to taste

Place all ingredients, except oil, in blender. Start blending and slowly add oil. Keep blending until emulsified. Season with salt and pepper to taste. Store in an airtight container in fridge for up to a week. Use pasteurized organic eggs to avoid using raw eggs.

Debbie Portell

Southern Saucy French Dressing

2/3 cup Red Wine Vinegar-of your choice
1/2 cup Extra Virgin Olive Oil
1 cup Bone Suckin Sauce

Mix together 2/3 cup red wine vinegar & 1/2 cup extra virgin olive oil in a container, shake/mix well. Mix 1/2 cup of well mixed red wine vinegar & extra virgin olive oil mixture with 1 cup of bone suckin sauce. Shake well & refrigerate!

Note: For a variation in taste, you can adjust the amounts of each ingredient to your tastebuds liking. You'll also find that you'll like it on more than just salads! Enjoy!!

John, Sophia & Jeanine Morris
2014

Debbie Portell & Tony Morris
2014

Paleo Italian Salad Dressing

*This tastes great as a marinade on chicken!

1 cup Olive Oil
1 cup Red Wine Vinegar (or experiment with a combo of other vinegars or lemon juice)
2 1/2 tsp Garlic Powder
2 tsp Onion Powder or Dried Minced Onion
2 1/2 tsp Dried Oregano
2 1/2 tsp Dried Basil
2 tsp Pepper
2 tsp Salt
2 tsp Dried or Prepared Mustard (take your pick)

Combine ingredients in a jar. Store tightly covered at room temperature or in the refrigerator (will need to let the olive oil come to room temp. before serving.) Shake well before pouring. Enjoy!

Michelle Swindle & Family
2014

Aimee Nassif & Kevin Carriker
2014

Garlic Green Beans

1 small package of microwavable Green Beans
Olive oil
Fresh garlic
Salt/pepper

Prepare green beans according to bag. Remove from microwave and place green beans into a bowl, and then run under cold water (this will stop them from continuing to cook as the bag will be hot). Meanwhile, drizzle olive oil in sauté pan and bring to low/medium heat. Mince fresh garlic (as much as you like) and place in the pan. Add the green beans and sprinkle lightly with salt/pepper. Place green beans in the pan, tossing occasionally, for approximately 3 minutes or until green beans are warm. For crunchier green beans, reduce the microwaving time by 1-2 minutes.

Serve with Aimee's Tuna Steak on page 84

Roasted Broccoli with Garlic

3 lbs. of Organic Broccoli, cut into bite sized flowerets
6 tbs Extra Virgin Olive Oil
9 fresh Garlic cloves
Sea Salt

Preheat oven to 400°. Cut broccoli into bite sized pieces. Slice garlic cloves into thin pieces.
Toss broccoli with olive oil, garlic & salt, then spread on a baking sheet. Roast until broccoli is bright green and edges are starting to brown slightly, 20-25 minutes. Serve hot.

Makes about 8 servings

Beverly Sloan
2014

Squash & Basil Soup

45 mins total 20 mins prep

1 1/2 - 1 3/4 lbs mixed Summer Squash
1 Onion
3 cloves Garlic
4 tbs Olive Oil
4 cups Homemade or Organic Vegetable Stock
1 cup fresh Basil
Sea Salt and freshly Ground Black Pepper, to taste

Roughly chop the washed squash, onion and garlic, then gently soften, part-covered, in the heated oil, stirring now and again (10 minutes). Pour in 4 cups of the stock and bring to a boil. Simmer uncovered for about 10 minutes. Add the basil leaves, then blend together (food processor or blender) until smooth with tiny flecks of basil visible. Season to taste. Enjoy hot or cold.

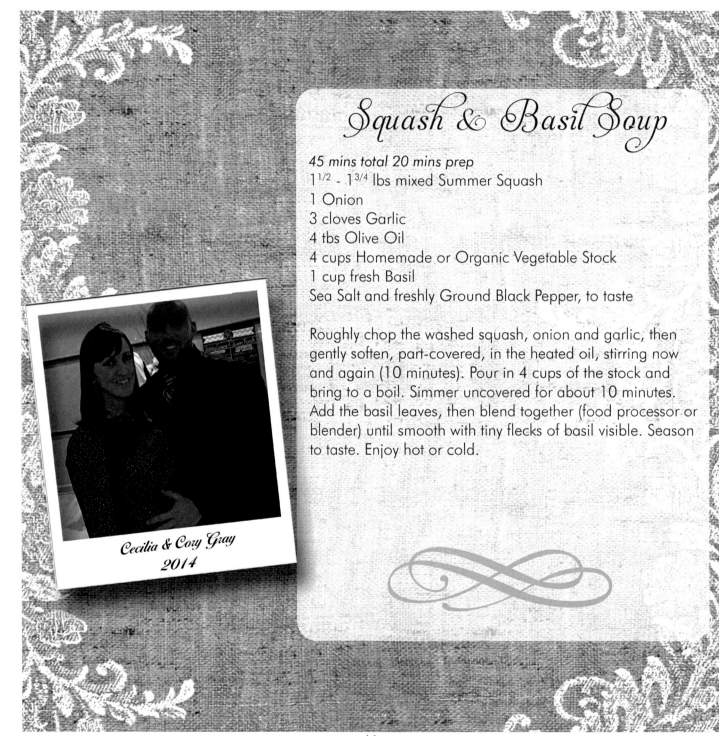

Cecilia & Cory Gray
2014

Mashed Sweet Potatoes

6 Medium Sweet Potatoes
Cinnamon & Stevia
1 tbsp Agave Nectar
1 tbsp Unsweetened Almond Milk

Preheat oven to 400° F, Wash sweet potatoes and lay on a cookie sheet. Bake for 90 minutes. Remove from oven and let cool. Peel off the skin and mash the sweet potatoes in a bowl. Add agave nectar, almond milk, and more cinnamon & stevia to taste. Blend with a hand mixer until smooth.

Cranberry Sauce

2 bags of Cranberries frozen or fresh
1 1/2 cups of water
1/2 cup of agave
1/2 cup of granulated Stevia
1/2 of juiced orange

Simmer on medium heat until all the cranberries pop. Keep stirring constantly until your desired thickness. I like to serve mine with toasted walnuts.

Debbie Portell & Sophia
2014

Molly
2014

Debbie Pastell & Sophia
2014

Sophia
2014

Molly
2014

Roasted Beets

14 Beets
3 tbsp Olive Oil
1 Shallot Chopped
2 tsp Sea Salt
1 tsp Pepper
2 tbsp Red Wine Vinegar
Juice of half Lemon
1 tbsp Stevia in the Raw

Remove top and root of beet and peel. Cut into chunks, place on sheet cake pan. Mix shallot, olive oil, salt and pepper. Roast 30-45 minutes or until desired doneness. Turn them midway. Immediately add vinegar, lemon, and stevia to the beets as you take them out of the oven. Serve over greens and top with either toasted walnuts or crumbled goat cheese.

Sophia
2014

Sophia & John Mozis
2014

Roasted Carrots

30 Organic Whole Carrots
3 tbsp Olive Oil
Stevia
Sea Salt & Pepper

Peel carrots. Slice diagonally into smaller, even pieces. Spread evenly on pan and sprinkle with Stevia, salt, pepper and olive oil. Roast in a 425°F oven for 40-50 minutes.

Roasted Brussels Sprouts

2 - 3 lbs. of Fresh Brussels Sprouts (cut in half)
1 large Shallot
1 tbsp Olive Oil
Sea Salt
Pepper
1 tbsp of Onion Powder
2 cloves of Garlic, minced

Saute shallot, garlic and olive oil. Roll fresh Brussels Sprouts in the mixture. Foil line a sheet cake pan, lay veggie mixture out evenly. Bake at 350° for 30 minutes, toss them around and cook 15 minutes more, or until desired doneness.

Deviled Eggs

2 dozen Hard Boiled Eggs
1 tsp Dry Mustard
1 tbsp Red Wine Vinegar
1 cup Mayo (see Debbie's Mayonnaise recipe on page 60)

Take all yolks and add to the mixer. Combine remaining ingredients and mix until well combined. Add extra mayo if needed. Salt and pepper to taste. Scoop into egg whites.

Debbie & Molly

Hearty Hefty Chili

1 Orange pepper
1 Red Pepper
1 large Onion
3 tbsp Chili Powder
2 tbsp Onion Powder
1 tbsp Sea Salt
2 tbsp Stevia
6 stalks of Celery
1 tbsp Franks Hot Sauce
2 cans of chopped Tomatoes
2 large cans of Tomato Sauce
3 lbs Ground Turkey or Bison
2 Green Pepper
1 Yellow Pepper
1/2 small can of Tomato Paste
1/4 cup Bone Sucking Sauce
1 tbsp Garlic Powder
2 tbsp Black Pepper
1 dash Cayenne
1 dash Red Pepper flakes

Chop and saute the veggies in olive oil, cook meat separately and drain. Add all ingredients together. Stir well, cook on medium for 30 minutes. tastes great served over roasted spaghetti squash.

John & Debbie
2014

Molly
2014

Hearty Vegetable Soup

6 cups Vegetable Stock or Bouillon
1 grounded cup Raw Cashews
1 medium Onion, finely chopped
2 Celery sticks , chopped
1 Garlic clove, minced
1/2 large Red Bell Pepper, chopped
2 medium unpeeled Potatoes, cubed
(substitute with Sweet Potatoes)
1 large head of Broccoli, including stem, chopped (4 cups)
2 tsp dried Thyme
1 tsp Sea Salt
1/2 tsp Black Pepper

Puree 1 cup of the vegetable stock with the cashews in a blender until smooth. Set aside. In a large pot, cook the onion, celery, and carrot over medium heat in 1 cup of the vegetable stock for 5 minutes. Add the garlic, bell pepper, and potatoes and cook for 2 more minutes. Add the remaining 4 cups of vegetable stock and the broccoli, thyme, salt, and black pepper, and bring to a boil over high heat. Cover and simmer until the broccoli and potatoes are soft, about 10 minutes. Add the cashew mixture to the soup ad stir until mixed. Remove the pot from heat and puree about half the soup, in small batches, until smooth. Return pureed soup to the pot and reheat, stirring well. Serve.

Elaine & Sandy
2014

Romaine Salad with Fresh Strawberries
and Strawberry Tarragon Dressing

Salad
1 large head of Romaine Lettuce, shredded
1 medium Red Onion, thinly sliced
2 sticks of Celery, chopped
1 pint of fresh Strawberries, hulled & cut in half

Mix all of the salad ingredients together in a large bowl. Toss the salad with Strawberry Tarragon Dressing to taste.

Serves 4 and makes enough dressing for 12. Serve with Elaine's Strawberry Tarragon Dressing on page 58.

Elaine & Monica
2014

Cauliflower 'Mashed Potatoes'

2 heads Cauliflower, core removed, cut into florets
1 tbs Olive Oil
4 cups Unsweetened Almond Milk
1 tsp Sea Salt
1/2 bunch Chives, minced for garnish

Preheat oven to 350° F. On a sheet tray, spread 1/4 of the florets with 1/2 of the oil, season with salt and bake until caramelized, about 25 minutes. Meanwhile, combine remaining cauliflower, almond milk and half a tsp of sea salt in a medium saucepan over medium heat. Bring mixture to a simmer, cover, and cook until cauliflower is tender, about 20 to 25 minutes. Strain cauliflower from milk mixture, reserving both. Transfer cauliflower to a blender. Add remaining 1/2 tsp of salt and 1/2 tbs of oil to the blender. Add half of the reserved milk liquid. Secure top on blender and puree mixture until smooth. If mixture is too thick, thin by adding some of the remaining liquid. Season, to taste. Serve in a large serving bowl topped with caramelized florets and chives.

Joe's wife, Kathleen & daughter, Gabrielle
2014

Meat & Veggie Chowder

1lb of Ground Turkey or Chicken
1lb of Ground Bison
1lb Ground Veal
2 tbsp Olive Oil
4 cloves of fresh Garlic, minced
1 large chopped Onion
3 Shallots, minced
1lb "box" Chicken or Turkey Broth, 99% fat free/low sodium
2+ cups Water
1/2 tsp Ground Pepper
1 tbsp Garam Masala Seasoning
2 tbsp dried Italian Seasoning (no salt)
2 tbsp Stevia
1 jar Bone Sucking Sauce
4+ cups chopped Veggies of choice (green beans, broccoli, cauliflower, kale, spinach, zucchini, yellow squash, mushroom and small amount of carrots for color)
3 stalks of Celery, chopped

add or delete spices depending on flavor of interest. Other ideas would be chipotle seasoning, cayenne pepper, or ginger.

Heat oil, garlic, shallots. Brown all three meats together in the oil. Once browned, add broth and all other spices. Simmer 10 minutes. Put in crock pot with all veggies and add water. Slow cook until veggies are tender.

Karen Schneider
2014

Chili

4 to 5 pounds Lean Ground Beef (browned and grease drained)
1 bunch of Celery (chopped)
3 Red Bell Peppers (chopped)
3 Green Bell Peppers (chopped)
2 large Onions
2 cans Rotel Original Tomatoes
3 cans Tomato Sauce
1 can Tomato Paste
6 cloves Garlic - minced or pressed
6 tbsp Chili Powder
4 tbsp Olive Oil
Sea Salt and Black Pepper to taste

Saute onion, peppers, celery and garlic in olive oil.
Add saute mixture to browned ground Beef (drain grease).
Add tomatoes, sauces and seasonings to taste.
Simmer on low for 2 hours until seasonings are baked in for maximum flavor.

Makes HEARTY chili, almost a dip-like consistency. I use celery sticks to dip and eat.

Jerome & Kim Simon
2014

Hearty Chili

Roasted Rosemary Sweet Potatoes

2 raw peeled Sweet Potatoes - 1" cubes
2 cloves Garlic - minced or pressed
2 tbsp fresh Rosemary - finely chopped
2 tbsp Olive Oil
Sea Salt and Black Pepper to taste

Preheat oven to 375° F. Line cookie sheet with foil. Cut peeled sweet potatoes into one-inch rounds to make them easier to cube. Place potato cubes in a medium mixing bowl. Add the olive oil, sea salt, pepper, garlic and rosemary and toss together. Spread out on foil-lined cookie sheet. Bake about 35 minutes - turn cubes over about 10 min before time is up.
(For crispy potatoes, turn broiler on for the final few minutes)

Jerome & Kim Simon
2014

Roasted Rosemary Sweet Potatoes
2014

Christmas Crunch Salad

4 cups Fresh Broccoli florets (3/4 pound)
4 cups Fresh Cauliflower florets (3/4 pound)
1 medium Red Onion, chopped
2 cups Cherry Tomatoes, halved

Dressing:
1 cup Mayonnaise (See Debbie's Mayo recipe on page 60)
1/2 cup Organic Sour cream
1 tbsp Stevia
1 tbsp vinegar
Pepper to taste

In a large salad bowl, combine vegetables. Whisk the dressing ingredients until smooth; pour over vegetables and toss to coat. Cover and chill at least 2 hours. Yield: 14 servings.

Kristen Kostner
2014

Leslie Moore

Farmer Girl Meats Sweet Potato Chili

I love this recipe because it's low-calorie yet chock-full of healthy, high fiber and high protein ingredients. The fiber comes from the veggies, the protein from our Farmer Girl grass-fed ground beef, raised right on my own farm.

1 pound Farmer Girl Lean Ground Beef
1 large Onion, chopped
1 large Sweet Potato, peeled and cubed
2 small Zucchini, diced
28 ounce can diced Tomatoes
1 small can Green Chillis
1 1/2 tbsp Chili Powder
1 tsp Cumin
1 tsp Salt
2 tsp Orange Zest
1/2 cup Vegetable Broth
1/2 to 1 cup of Chicken or Vegetable Stock
Parmesan cheese, grated

Brown ground beef with onion in large soup pot over medium heat until beef has lost pink color. Add chopped veggies and ingredients to broth. Bring to a boil. Add 1/2 to 1 cup chicken or vegetable stock. Decrease temperature to low simmer; continue cooking until sweet potatoes are soft, approximately 2 hours. Top with sprinkle of Parmesan cheese.

Farmer Girl Meats Sweet Potato Chili

Leslie Moore
Owner of Farmer Girl Meats

Spaghetti Squash

1 Spaghetti Squash
3 tbsp Olive Oil
2 tsp Garlic Powder
2 tsp Onion Powder
2 tsp Sea Salt
2 tsp Lemon Pepper
1 tsp Black Pepper

Microwave squash for 5 minutes to soften, cut in half and remove seeds from squash. Brush cut sides with 1 tbsp of olive oil, bake at 450° for 45 minutes, cut-side down on a foil lined cookie sheet. When done, let cool and remove squash. Add 2 tbsp olive oil, garlic powder, onion powder, sea salt, lemon pepper and black pepper.

Eric Ogden & Lisa Klaus
2014

Basic Cilantro Cauli-Rice

1 head Cauliflower
1 tbsp Coconut Oil
Sea Salt & Black Pepper to taste
1/4 cup finely chopped fresh Cilantro leaves
Optional add-ins: 1/4 cup minced Red Onion,
1/4 cup minced Yellow Bell Pepper, 1 tbsp Coconut Oil

Remove the outer leaves and stem from the cauliflower, and chop it into large chunks. Shred the cauliflower using a box grater or food processor. *If adding red onion and yellow bell pepper, saute the onion and pepper in the 1 tbsp of coconut oil over medium heat for about 5 minutes or until they become soft and have golden brown edges.*
In a large skillet over medium heat, melt the coconut oil and place the shredded cauliflower in the skillet. Add salt and pepper to taste. Saute for about 5 minutes or until the cauliflower begins to become translucent, stirring gently to ensure that it cooks through.
Stir in the optional add-ins (if using), place the cooked cauliflower in a serving bowl, and toss with the chopped cilantro before serving.

Maribel Hernandez
2014

Healthy Chicken Soup

10-12 cups Homemade broth (or canned if you didn't make while you cooked the chicken)
2 cups shredded Roasted Chicken (leftover from the roasted chicken you used to make broth or a store bought rotisserie)
4 Carrots, sliced diagonally ¼"
3 stalks Celery, thinly sliced
6-7 New Rose Potatoes, diced ½" or substitute Sweet Potatoes
1-14 oz can Diced Tomatoes
1 cup fresh or frozen Peas or 2 cups Green Beans
1 can Artichoke Hearts, packed in water, drained and quartered
1 small White or Yellow Onion, diced
1/8 - 1/4 tsp Cayenne Pepper
(start with 1/8 tsp and taste before adding more)
Sea salt, to taste
Freshly Ground Pepper
2 tbsp freshly chopped Parsley

Bring chicken broth to a simmer. Add carrots, celery, onions and parsley to broth. Simmer for 5 minutes. Add potatoes, then simmer for 10-12 more minutes or until a fork can easily pierce vegetables but they are still firm (no mushy veggies!) Add fresh or frozen peas or substitute with green beans, artichoke hearts, diced chicken and tomatoes. Turn off heat. Let sit for a few minutes so peas and chicken warm up. Add freshly turned pepper, cayenne pepper and sea salt, stir. Taste, make adjustments until you are happy. Serve. I like to freeze leftovers in individual sized containers so I always have a healthy soup on hand when I have little time to cook!

Roger Semsch
2014

Main Dishes

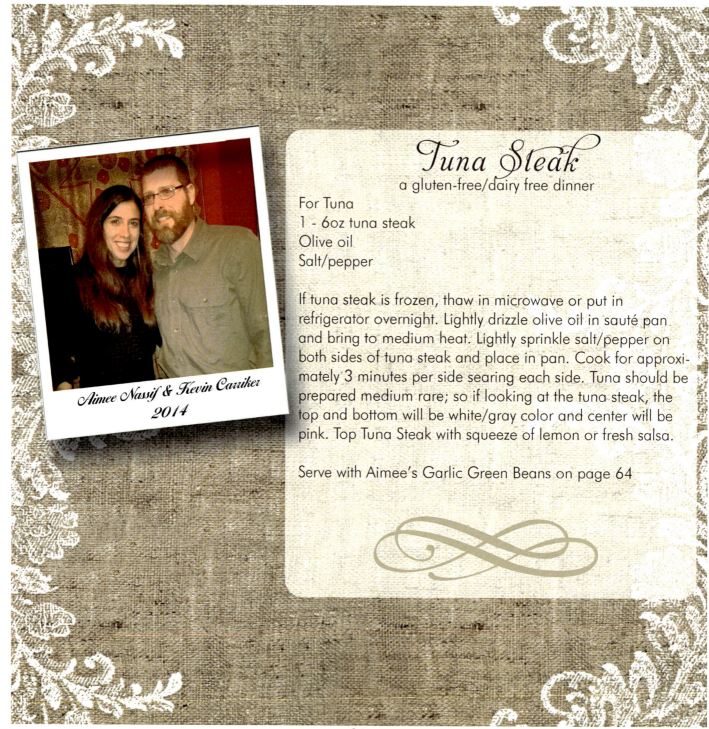

Tuna Steak
a gluten-free/dairy free dinner

For Tuna
1 - 6oz tuna steak
Olive oil
Salt/pepper

If tuna steak is frozen, thaw in microwave or put in refrigerator overnight. Lightly drizzle olive oil in sauté pan and bring to medium heat. Lightly sprinkle salt/pepper on both sides of tuna steak and place in pan. Cook for approximately 3 minutes per side searing each side. Tuna should be prepared medium rare; so if looking at the tuna steak, the top and bottom will be white/gray color and center will be pink. Top Tuna Steak with squeeze of lemon or fresh salsa.

Serve with Aimee's Garlic Green Beans on page 64

Aimee Nassif & Kevin Carriker
2014

Meatloaf

Gluten-free, dairy free

1lb lean Grass fed Ground Beef
1/2 medium Yellow Onion, diced
1 Egg (organic/free range)
1 cup Crispy Brown Rice Cereal (I use Erewhon Organic)
1 tbsp Gluten-free Worcestershire Sauce
(most brands are already gluten free)
2 tbsp Organic All-Natural Ketchup
1 tsp Pink Himalayan Salt
1 tsp Black Pepper

Sauce
4 tbsp Organic All-Natural Ketchup
1 1/2 tbsp Apple Cider Vinegar
1 tbsp Real Maple Syrup

Combine all the ingredients for the meatloaf together, mixing well. Place in greased loaf 9x5 loaf pan. Mix all the sauce ingredients and spread over the top of the uncooked meatloaf
Bake at 325° for 45 min-1 hour

Serves 4-6

Ben Lueken & Caity Hawksley
2014

Steak Kabobs

1/3 cup Olive Oil
1/3 cup Coconut Aminos
¼ tsp Garlic Powder
1¼ lb Fillet Tenderloin cut into cubes
Cracked black pepper

Cut tenderloin into cubes, add first 3 items in bowl and marinate 24 hrs. Take tenderloin and make kabobs out of them and then season with black pepper.
Grill to desired temp.

Kim Simon, Joy Thornton & Cadwallader
2014

Chicken Veggetti

(Veggetti; shredder found at Bed Bath and Beyond)

Serving Size: 2 portions
2-8oz. Chicken breast (boneless & skinless)
½ cup Gluten-Free Bread Crumbs
2 tbs Olive Oil
4 med. Zucchini (2-green & 2-yellow)
1 large Tomato (vine ripened for added flavor)
¼ cup fresh Basil (chopped)
1 tbs minced Garlic
Cracked black pepper
Parmesan cheese

Place bread crumbs in a shallow dish and put 1 Tbs. of olive oil in separate dish. Lightly coat chicken breast in olive oil and then dredge in bread crumbs until lightly dusted. Grill chicken 3-4 minute per side or until done. Place in oven to keep warm. Dice large tomato and place in a mixing bowl. Chop fresh basil and add to tomatoes along with garlic and olive oil. Mix lightly. Remove vine end of zucchini then twist through the "thin" side of the Veggetti. Heat 1 tbs of olive oil in large skillet; med./high heat. Saute zucchini until soft approx. 3-5 min. Place bed of shredded zucchini on plate and top with chicken breast. Top chicken with 2-3 tablespoons of tomato/basil mixture.
*Cracked black pepper and parmesan to taste.

The Mantia Family

Sweet Garlic Chicken

Servings: 4
Serving Size: 1 chicken breast
Nutritional Information: Carbs 17g, Protein 28g, Fat <1g, Sugars 17g, Sodium 68mg

1.5 lbs boneless, skinless Chicken breast (4 pieces)
4 tsp Garlic, minced
3 tbsp Organic Agave Nectar (or Agave equiv)
3 tsp Olive Oil

Preheat oven to 375°. Arrange the chicken in square baking dish. Season if desired. Stir Agave, olive oil and garlic together, along with any spices you desire. Pour over chicken. Bake for 30-45 minutes until chicken is just cooked. (cooking times may vary) Turn oven to BROIL. Sprinkle Stevia over top of chicken. Broil for 3-5 minutes until Stevia caramelizes.

Optional: Squeeze fresh lemon over chicken and season to taste.

Dave DeRemer
2014

Fajita Chicken

Barbara & Bill Clark

1/2 cup Olive Oil
2 tbsp Annie's Worcestershire Sauce
Juice of 1 whole Lime
3 Garlic cloves, minced
3 tbsp Chili Powder
1 tsp Red Pepper Flakes
1 tsp Sea Salt
1/2 tbsp Black Pepper
8 Chicken breasts

Place 8 chicken breasts in large 9x13 container. Set aside. Take all remaining ingredients and blend them together in a blender until well combined. Pour over chicken and allow chicken to marinate in sauce. Grill each breast. Serve 1/2 avocado over the top with salsa. Taste great to top a salad with.

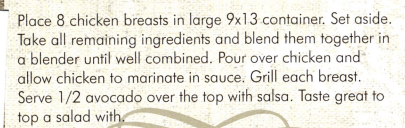
Bill, Debbie & Molly

Slow Cooked Turkey Breast

4 Turkey Breast tenderloins
1 bundle of Celery chopped
1 large White Onion chopped
1 tbsp granulated Garlic
1 tbsp granulated Onion
1 tbsp Oregano
Sea Salt and Pepper to taste

Place turkey breast in crock pot. Add chopped celery and onion to the turkey mix. Fill the crock pot up with water to the top fully submerging the turkey with water. Cook on low for 8 hours. Drain into a strainer and shred inside an 9x13 pan. Mixing the veggies in with it as you shred it. Add all seasoning and combine with Turkey and veggies. Tastes great alone, in a lettuce wrap with spicy mustard, or on top of a salad.

John Morris & Debbie Portell
2014

Roasted Butternut Squash, Pears, & Walnuts

1/2 tsp of Stevia Powdered Extract or
12 to 18 drops of Stevia Liquid Concentrate
1/2 tsp of Cinnamon
1/4 tsp ground Ginger
1/4 tsp Nutmeg
1/4 tsp ground Cloves
2 pinches of Kosher Salt
4 cups of Butternut Squash cut into 1 inch cubes
3 cups of Bartlett Pears cut into 1 inch cubes
1/2 cup of Walnuts, chopped
2 tbsp Olive Oil or Coconut Oil

Preheat oven to 350 degrees. In a small bowl, stir together stevia, cinnamon, ginger, nutmeg, cloves, and salt. Set aside. In a large bowl, toss together butternut squash, pears, and walnuts. Pour olive or coconut oil over it and sprinkle with stevia/spice mix. Toss until well distributed. Spread into a 9×13 baking dish and bake for 30 minutes. Remove from oven and toss. Return to the oven for another 15 minutes, or until the squash and pears are tender. Serve hot and Enjoy!

Dee Dee Fetouh
2014

Caribbean Tilapia & Green Beans

Jessica Revere & Family
2014

5oz Tilapia
Mrs. Dash Caribbean Citrus Blend
Steam in bag Green Beans
1 tbsp Olive Oil

Brush tilapia with olive oil and season tilapia with Mrs. Dash Seasoning. Place tilapia on foil that has been brushed with olive oil to prevent sticking. Bake in oven at 350° for 20 mins or until desired doneness. Cook Green beans according to package instructions. Remove and season with Mrs. Dash Caribbean Citrus blend.

Chicken & Spaghetti Squash

3 1/2 lb Spaghetti Squash
2 tbsp Olive Oil
2 tbsp Almond flour
2 ounces or 1 whole skinless boneless Chicken breast (cut into 1/2" cubes)
1/2 cup (packed) Fresh Parsley or Basil Leaves
1/2 cup Almond Milk
1 cup chicken broth
1 Garlic clove
Salt
1/2 cup freshly grated Parmesan

Preheat the oven to 375°. With a sharp knife, prick the squash in 2 - 3 places and place on a baking pan. Bake for 30 minutes. Remove from oven, cut it in half lengthwise and scoop out the seeds. Return the squash halves, cut side down, to the baking sheet and bake for another 30 minutes or until tender.

While the squash is cooking, heat the olive oil in a medium sized saucepan. Add the almond flour and cook for 1 minute, stirring continuously. Add the garlic, broth and bring the mixture to a boil, whisking all the while. Add the chicken and simmer, uncovered, for 3 to 5 minutes or until chicken is cooked through. Remove from the heat and stir in the Almond milk. Season with 1 tsp of salt and pepper to taste; set aside and reheat over low heat when you remove the squash from the oven.

Remove the squash from the oven. With a fork rake the squash until it separates fully into strands and only the shell remains. Transfer the strands to pasta bowls. Remove the chicken sauce from the heat, stir in the cheese and parsley or basil and adjust the seasoning. Serve the sauce over the strands of squash

Joe, Kathleen & Gabrielle
2014

Bbq Hamburger & Rice

5 lbs of Ground Sirloin
1 large Onion, chopped
1 tbsp Onion Powder
1 jar of Bone Suckin' Sauce
1 tbsp Sea Salt
1 tbsp Black Pepper
Whole Grain Brown Rice

Brown ground sirloin. Add chopped onion, onion powder, garlic powder, sea salt and black pepper. Drain well. Add $1^{1/2}$ jars bone suckin' bbq sauce and 6 cups of brown rice.

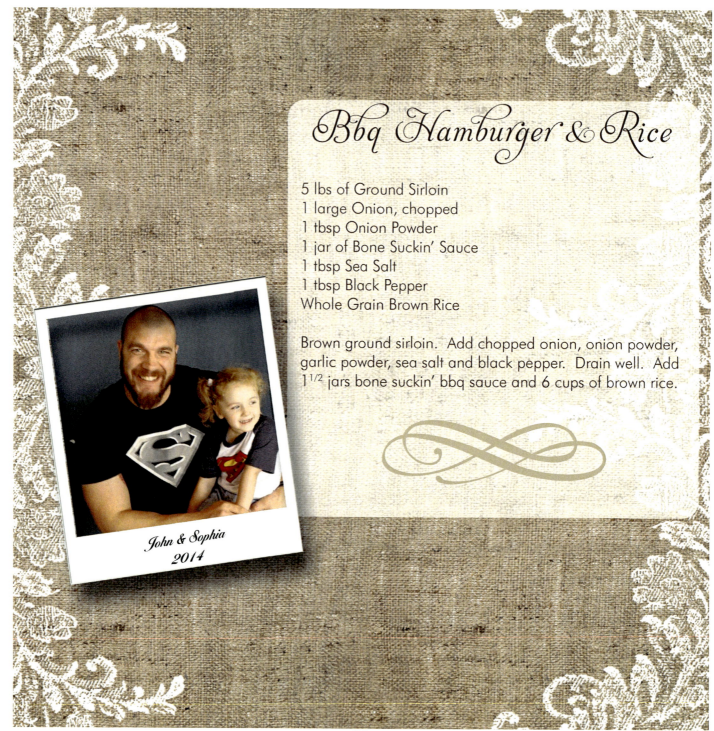

John & Sophia
2014

Red Hot Chicken

10 - 12 boneless skinless chicken breasts
2 bottles of Frank's Red Hot Sauce
4 cups of Whole Grain Brown Rice
Large Crock Pot

Rinse and place chicken breast in large crock pot. Pour 1 bottle of Frank's Red Hot sauce over chicken evenly. Cook on low for 10-12 hours. I prefer 12 hours. Drain chicken well. Place in a 13" x 9" pan. Use two forks and shred the chicken well. Pour the 2nd bottle of Frank's Red Hot sauce over the chicken and stir well. Add 4 cups of whole grain rice, stir and serve.

Sophia & Tony Morris
2014

John, Debbie & Tony
2014

Beef Roast with Apples

24 oz Beef Sirloin Roast (lean)
1 tbsp Garlic Powder
1 small chopped Red Onion
1 tbsp Cinnamon
1 tsp Apple Pie Spice
1 Apple with skin, sliced
1 - 2 cups water
Add 2 cups Baby Carrots (Optional)

Add all ingredients to your roaster or crock pot. Top with Apples. Bake until tender.

Serves 6
Calories 125, Carbs 5, Fat 4, Protein 17, Sugar 3

The Lipe Family

Avocado Chicken Salad

2 - 3 boneless, skinless Chicken Breasts
2 Avocados (peeled, pitted & mashed)
1 chopped Celery Stick
2 tbsp chopped Cilantro
1 Lime
Hot Sauce

Cook chicken in crock pot, shred after cooking. Add mashed avocado, celery & cilantro. Squeeze lime juice and add zest. Top with your favorite hot sauce to taste.

Lisa Klaus, Michaela Huff and Mary Klaus
2014

Perfectly Browned Oven Roasted Turkey

Lisa & Eric
2014

Turkey, size of your choosing.
Hint (Do not scrimp on the quality of the bird)
Cheese cloth – 4 layers and large enough to cover entire bird
4-6 Jonathan or similar tart Apples quartered
3 sticks Unsalted Butter
Olive oil
Ground sage
Dried Rosemary
Large roasting pan with rack

Remove the giblet pack. Rinse turkey under cold running water making sure body cavity is well rinsed and drained. Pat dry with paper towels making sure liquid is out of body cavity. Dampen paper towel with olive oil and wipe inside of bird. This is more easily done with the bird standing. Shake the ground sage and rosemary liberally into body cavity making sure all sides are coated. Stuff the body cavity with the quartered apples until full. Rub the skin with 1 stick of softened butter until the skin glistens. Shake the sage and rosemary over the entire bird making sure it is coated well. Place on rack in roasting pan

Pre-heat oven to 350°.
Melt 2 sticks of butter in a flat pan. Once melted, place cheese cloth in it and allow it to soak up the butter for 5 minutes. Once cheese cloth has soaked up the butter, raise it up out of the pan and gently ring out lightly to remove excess. Save the melted butter that is left for basting. Drape the cheese cloth over the bird, making sure to cover it completely.
Place bird in oven, set timer for 30 minutes. Baste the cheese cloth on the bird with the saved melted butter and return to oven, continuing to baste in this manor every 30 minutes. Check the temp. with a meat thermometer in the breast and thigh after 2 ½ hours and then continue cooking until the bird has reached 180°. Once 180° has been reached, remove the bird from oven and remove the cheese cloth and dispose.
Allow bird to stand for 10 minutes, then remove the apples from the body cavity and dispose. Your golden brown bird is now ready to be admired and carved!

Pan Seared Tilapia with Fresh Veggies

Megan

Rustin Raleigh & Megan Kenkel 2014

4 thawed or fresh Tilapia fillets
Chopped fresh Cucumber, Tomato, and Celery
Garlic Powder
Italian Seasoning
Sea salt
Pepper
Olive oil

Pour enough Olive oil in bottom of pan, to just cover the bottom so fish doesn't stick. Place 4 Tilapia fillets in pan on medium low heat. Drizzle fish with olive oil, sprinkle with garlic powder, Italian seasoning, sea salt and pepper. Cover pan and cook for 2-3 minutes. Then add fresh chopped cucumber, tomato, and celery. Cook Tilapia till flaky in texture, all while veggies simmer in now seasoned olive oil. Serve and enjoy this healthy yet time efficient recipe.

Turkey & Tomato Stuffed Mushrooms

4 Portobello Mushrooms
4 cloves of Garlic
1 1/2 lbs Ground Turkey
1 tsp Fennel
1 tsp Oregano
1/2 tsp Basil
1 can Artichoke Hearts chopped
1 Onion diced
1 jar sundried Tomatoes (in olive oil) drained & chopped or roasted Tomatoes
1 large tub Spinach (4-5 cups) torn into pieces
1/2 cup Mayonnaise
(See Debbie's Mayonnaise recipe on page 60)

Peel and dice garlic, saute and dice onions. Cook turkey, add in fennel, oregano & basil. Combine into one large skillet. Add artichokes, tomatoes and spinach to skillet. Saute for 3 minutes. Remove from heat, stir in mayo. Divide mixture into the 4 mushroom caps. Bake at 400° for 12 minutes.

Melissa Lafferty & Family
2014

Dijon Almond Crusted Tilapia

2 Tilapia Fillets (approx. 1lb.)
1/2 cup Whole Raw Almonds
1/4 cup Dijon Mustard
1 tsp Smoked Paprika
Salt and Pepper to taste
Coconut Oil for pan frying

Chop almonds fine in food processor. Transfer nuts to dish with paprika and mix. Season fillets generously with salt and pepper. Spread mustard on both sides of fillet and coat with almond mixture. Heat oil in skillet over med heat. When hot place fillets in skillet & Cook 3 minutes each side.
May need to cook longer due to thickness and size of fillet.

Michelle Swindle & Family
2014

Crock Pot Turkey Meatballs in Tomato Spinach Sauce

Olive Oil or Olive Oil Sprayed from Misto
2 lb Ground Turkey
1 large Onion, finely diced
1 lb chopped Spinach
(I use frozen, but fully defrosted)
28 oz can Crushed Tomatoes
2 tsp Kosher salt, add more to taste
1 tsp Garlic Powder
1 tsp Onion Powder
1/2 tsp Cumin
1/2 tsp Paprika
1 tsp Oregano
Pinch Red Pepper Flakes
1/2 cup water

Mike Harris
2014

Heat or spray oil in a large frying pan. Form the turkey into balls (it will be hard to work with, so don't worry if they aren't perfect balls). Fry in hot frying pan on all sides until they are browned. The middles will still be raw, but they will cook in the sauce, so that's fine. Don't overcrowd the pan, rather work in batches. Remove the meatballs from the pan and place in the pot of your crockpot. Add a bit more oil to the pan, and add the diced onions. Next, add the chopped spinach and sauté for a few minutes. Pour the vegetable mixture over the meatballs in the crock pot.

Pour the crushed tomatoes over into the crockpot. Add the spices and water. Stir the entire mixture gently, being careful not to break up the meatballs.

Cook the meatballs in the crock pot on low for at least six hours. Serve hot over brown rice or brown rice pasta.

Integrity Stuffed Peppers

4 large Peppers (choice of colors)
1 lb of meat (Ground Turkey or Ground Bison)
1 can of diced Tomatoes
2 cloves of minced Garlic
1 small chopped Onion
1/2 to 1 tbs of Hot Sauce (more or less to taste)
Pepper (to taste)

Preheat oven to 325°. Add meat, garlic, onion, hot sauce, and pepper in saute pan and brown. Once meat is browned add tomatoes and simmer. Cut tops off peppers and remove seeds, place in square baking dish. Stuff peppers with meat mixture and cover with foil (I have also added a slice of tomato to the top of each pepper as "a lid" sprinkled with chili powder as an option)
Bake for about 30 minutes or until peppers are tender.

Mike Meyer
2014

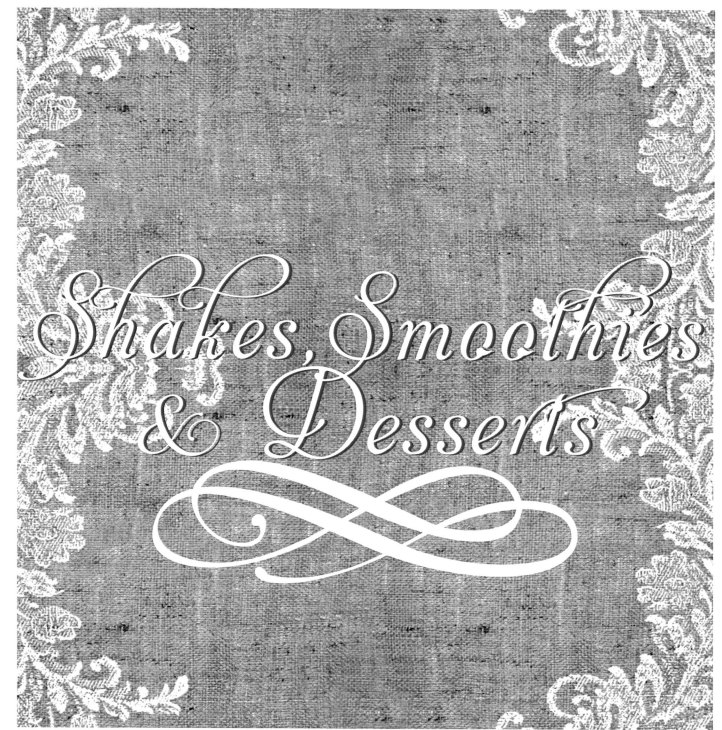

Shakes, Smoothies & Desserts

The Balanced Power Shake

handful of Spinach
handful of Ice
handful of Blueberries
1 tbsp Almond Butter or Natural Peanut Butter
1 scoop of Whey or Egg White Protein, flavor of choice
(I like chocolate by Beverly International)
8 oz of Whole Milk or Water
(depending on calorie preference & thickness of Shake)
Flaxseed (optional)
Glutamine (optional)

Blend and enjoy!

Adam & Natalie
2014

Adam, Nolan & Riley Coffey
2014

Nutty Coconut Butter Bars
-HOLD THE INFLAMMATION

1/2 cup Almond Meal (or finely ground almonds)
1 cup chopped Pecans
1 cup Enjoy Life Dark Chocolate Morsels
1 cup chopped Walnuts
1/2 cup Pepitas (pumpkin seeds)
1/2 cup raw Sunflower Seeds
2/3 cup Roasty Toasty Coconut Butter
3/4 cup Almond Butter
1 1/2 tsp Vanilla Extract
1/2 tsp Sea Salt

Preheat oven at 350°. Combine the first six ingredients and salt in a large bowl. Warm almond butter, add vanilla and mix completely. Pour over the nut mixture and stir until thoroughly coated. If any of the ingredients are still dry, add additional almond butter to coat completely. Warm coconut butter and incorporate into the mixture.
Line an 9x13 baking dish with parchment paper and press the mixture into the pan. Use a rolling pin or glass to pack it tightly so the bars will stay together after baking. Bake at 350° until the edges are golden (12-15 minutes). Remove from the oven and let cool completely before cutting with a sharp knife. Store at room temperature.

Angie Carl & Family
2014

2014

Pumpkin Pie Pecan Mousse

1 (15 oz.) can of Organic Pure Pumpkin
1 container Whipped topping, thawed
1/4 cup Stevia or natural sweetener of your choice
1/2 tbsp Vanilla extract
Crushed Pecans for garnish

Combine all ingredients except pecans until well mixed & fluffy. Fill serving bowls evenly and top with crushed pecans. Serve chilled.

(Serves 4)

Beverly & Mike Sloan
2014

Cindy's Protein Pancakes

Serving Size: 4 pancakes

12 Egg Whites
½ cup Vanilla Protein powder
½ cup Oats
¼ cup chopped Walnuts
1 cup unsweetened Blueberries (fresh or frozen)

Combine all ingredients in mixing bowl and mix together. Heat medium skillet sprayed with Pam cooking spray. Place ¼ of mixture in skillet and cook until golden brown on both sides.

Gus & Cindy Mantia
2014

Hulk and Dan Hoormann
2014

Dan's Weight Gainer Shake

Due to certain stomach issues and a very hyper active metabolism it was very hard for me to eat and maintain weight. Eating the foods that I liked on a regular basis would often be cause for stomach issues. After talking to Debbie, I realized there were a few trigger foods to stay away from and ideas of other foods that would allow me to eat on a regular basis preventing stomach issues. These would also allow me to workout, eat the correct amount, allow me to recover and to gain muscle, as it was my goal. Now as part of my daily meal plan I incorporate 2 shakes a day, which give me the calories and protein I need for my lifestyle, since I am what people would call a hard gainer.

My shakes include:

1/2 cup of Gluten-Free Oatmeal
1 scoop of Jay Robb Chocolate Protein
1 tbsp spoon of Hemp Oil
1 tbsp of Coconut Oil
1 tbsp of Chia Seeds
1 tbsp of MCT oil
16 ounces of Water

This shake gives me an extra 700 calories per shake, plus the health and energy benefits have been great. Of course it can be scaled down for half the measurements if you don't need that many calories.

Gluten-Free Pumpkin Pie

Filling:
- 2 Eggs
- 1/2 tsp Nutmeg
- 1 tsp Cinnamon
- 1/8 tsp Ginger
- 1 can Pumpkin
- 1 cup Unsweetened Vanilla Almond Milk
- 1/2 tsp Salt
- 1/2 cup Stevia in the Raw
- 2 tbsp Dark Agave
- 1/4 tsp Cloves (if you like the spice)
- 1/4 cup chopped pecans

Crust:
- 1 cup Whole Gluten Free Oats
- 1 cup Ground Almonds
- 1 tbsp Stevia
- 1 tsp Cinnamon
- 1/4 cup chopped pecans
- 1 tbsp Coconut Oil melted

Mix pie mixture in mixer, set aside. Melt coconut oil. Combine remaining ingredients and form into a crumb crust at the bottom of a greased 8x8 pan with coconut oil. Press into the bottom of the pan into a crust. A pie pan can be used as well. Pour pumpkin mixture on top of crust. Bake at 350° oven for 45 minutes to an hour or until set. Cool for an hour then cut.

John Morris & Debbie Portell 2014

Molly 2014

John, Sophia & Debbie 2014

Peanut Butter Protein Cookies

1 cup Smuckers All Natural Peanut Butter
1/2 cup Baking Stevia
1 whole large Egg
1 tsp Alcohol-Free Vanilla
1 tsp Aluminum-Free Baking Powder
1 tsp Cinnamon
1 tbsp Vanilla Jay Robb Protein Powder
1 whole mashed Banana
1 tbsp Agave

Combine all ingredients into a large bowl. Mix with whisk or hand mixer until well blended. Use small ice cream scoop to spread evenly distributed cookies across parchment paper or lined cookie sheet. Bake at 350° for 10-12 minutes. Should make 16 bite sized cookies.

Debbie & Sophia
2014

Jeri's Pumpkin Indulgence Smoothie

1 cup Unsweetened Vanilla Almond Milk
1 scoop Jay Robb Vanilla Egg White Protein Powder
1 cup fresh Spinach
¼ cup Pumpkin Puree
1 tbsp All Natural Almond Butter (no sugar added)
1 tsp Cinnamon
Nutmeg, dash
Clove, dash
Ice, as desired

Blend all ingredients in blender on high. Enjoy!

Favorite Quote: "What you get by achieving your goals is not as important as what you become by achieving your goals."
— Henry David Thoreau

Ken's Strawberry Power Smoothie

1 scoop Jay Robb Vanilla Egg White Protein Powder
1 cup Strawberries
1 cup Water
1 tbsp Flax Oil (mixed berries flavor or plain)
Ice, as desired

Blend all ingredients in blender on high. Enjoy!

Jeri Madison
2014

Ken Madison
2014

Jeri's Yogurt Delight

½ cup Plain Yogurt (I use goat yogurt)
½ scoop Jay Robbs Chocolate Egg White Protein Powder
1 tbsp chopped Walnuts (or 2 teaspoons sliced almonds)
½ cup berries

Mix yogurt and protein powder until well blended. Stir in nuts and berries. Makes a great mid-morning or mid-afternoon snack.

Jeri Madison
2014

Apple Oatmeal

1 cup Oats
1 tbsp Natural Peanut Butter
1/2 chopped Apple
1 tbsp Stevia

Cook oats according to directions. Add remaining ingredients, stir and serve.

Sophia
2014

Sophia & John
2014

Caramel Apple Crisp

2 medium Apples
4 tbsp Torani Sugar Free Caramel Syrup
2 tbsp Walden Farms Caramel Dip
1/2 cup Almond Meal
1/2 Cup Fiber One Original Bran Cereal
2 tbsp" I Can't Believe it not Butter light"

Slice up apples and place in 8x8 pan. Stir in caramel syrup and caramel dip. Microwave for 5 minutes, until apples are tender. In the meantime, grind up Fiber one cereal in blender. Mix together the blended bran cereal with almond meal and sprinkle on top of apples. Drizzle with melted butter. Bake at 350 for 10 - 15 minutes.

Serves 9
Calories 69, Carbs 7g, Fat 5g, Protein 2g, Sugar 3g

Curtis & Kim Lipe

Zucchini Ice Cream Smoothie

1 cup of frozen Zucchini
1/2 cup Unsweetened Almond Breeze Milk
1 scoop of Protein Powder (any flavor)

Blend in blender until smooth..(may add more milk if needed)

Kim Lipe

Yogurt Parfait

1 cup plain Yogurt (Almond or Coconut)
1/2 scoop Jay Robb Strawberry Egg White Protein Powder
Stevia to taste
1/4 cup Blueberries
1/2 cup Strawberries sliced

Mix yogurt, protein powder and Stevia until well blended. Layer mixture with berries and enjoy.

Yogurt Parfait, submitted by Kim Simon

Protein Pumpkin Bread

1 1/2 cups Pure Pumpkin
1 cup Egg Whites
2 scoops Protein Powder
1/4 cup Flax Meal
1 tsp Baking Soda
3 tsp Cinnamon
1/2 tsp Nutmeg
2 packs Stevia

Bake in 4 mini loaf pans at 300° for 30 minutes.
4 servings

150 calories; 25 grams protein; 12 grams carbs
Less than 1 gram fat

Lisa & Debbie

Gluten-Free Apple Crisp

Serves 4 to 6
Filling:
6 medium Apples, peeled, cored, and diced
1 tsp Cinnamon
2 tbs Agave
1 tsp Lemon Juice

For the topping:
1/2 cup Almond Flour
1/2 cup Gluten-free Whole Oats
1/4 tsp Salt
1 tsp Cinnamon
1/4 cup Pecans, chopped
1/4 cup Stevia
2 tbsp Agave
1 tbsp Coconut Oil

Preheat oven to 375° F. In a medium bowl, combine the apples, 1 teaspoon cinnamon, 2 tablespoons honey, and lemon juice. Stir together until apples are coated evenly.
In a separate bowl, whisk together the almond flour, oats, salt, remaining cinnamon, and pecans.
Use a fork or your fingers (it's messy, but effective) to mix in the remaining stevia, agave and coconut oil, until the topping has a crumbly consistency.
Arrange the apples into a 9-inch pie dish or baking dish. Cover with the crumble topping.
Bake for 30 to 35 minutes, or until the top is golden brown. Remove from the oven and cool for 5 to 10 minutes.
Apple crisp is best served immediately, when it's warm. It can also be served at room temperature. Store, covered, in the refrigerator up to four days.

Misti Weatherfod & Family
2014

Clean Microwave Chocolate Mug Cake

in 5 minutes

This is a clean, healthy, low carb, protein and fiber rich cake in a mug. Healthy ingredients are used in this recipe to satisfy your sweet tooth and will not pack on calories.

1 tbsp Coconut Flour
1 tbsp Cocoa
1/4 tsp Baking Soda
1 Egg (or 2 tbsp Coconut Oil)
1 tbsp Agave (or honey)
1/2 Vanilla pod, seeds removed or 1/2 tsp of Vanilla Essence
3 tbsp Coconut Milk/ Almond Milk (or 3 tbsp water)
Sprinkle of Chocolate Chips (optional)

Note: Substitute 1/4 cup of mashed sweet potato for the egg. Also, added a pinch of cinnamon to enhance the chocolate flavor.

Place the dry ingredients to a microwave proof mug & combine well. Add the wet ingredients taking care to incorporate fully for a smooth mixture. Microwave on full power for $1^{1/2}$ minutes. Take out & enjoy from the mug or empty into a bowl.

Cook at less time for gooey consistency.

Fred & Monica
2014

Brown Rice Flour Tortilla Cinnamon Crisps

The Summers Family

Natasha & Chuck Summers 2014

1 1/2 cups Gluten Free Brown Rice Flour
1/2 cup Arrowroot Powder or Tapioca Flour
1/2 tsp Sea Salt
1 cup boiling water
Virgin Coconut Oil, for cooking
Cinnamon & Stevia

In a bowl, whisk together brown rice flour, arrowroot, and sea salt. Add the water, mix with a wooden spoon. Knead the dough a little in the bowl, let it rest while the skillet heats up. Add more water, 1 tbsp at a time, if the dough feels dry.

Preheat a 10-inch cast-iron skillet over medium heat. Divide the dough into six equal-sized balls. Place 1 rolled ball between 2 sheets of unbleached parchment paper, press and form a thin round tortilla, repeat.

Add about 1 tsp of coconut oil to the hot skillet. Gently remove the top sheet of parchment, place the tortilla into skillet, remove the second sheet of parchment. Cook for 1 to 2 minutes on each side. Repeat making tortillas with the remaining dough. Transfer the cooked tortillas to a plate, roll into pinwheels. Take melted coconut oil and brush it on the tortillas, roll tortillas in stevia and cinnamon mixture. Place on a cookie sheet and bake at 350° for 10 minutes or until crunchy.

You can also eliminate the stevia, cinnamon and baking steps to use for soft shell tacos or as wraps.

Yield: about 6 tortillas

No Bake Treats

1 cup (Dry) Gluten-free Old Fashioned Oats
2/3 cup Toasted No Sugar Added Coconut Flakes
1/2 cup Almond Butter
1/2 cup Ground Flaxseed
1/2 cup Carob Chips (find at Whole Foods)
1/3 cup Coconut Oil
1tsp Chia Seeds
1tsp Vanilla Extract

Combine all ingredients in a med size bowl stir until well mixed. Cover and let chill in refrigerator for half an hour. Once chilled roll into balls of whatever size you would like. Mine were about 1" in diameter. Store in an airtight container and keep refrigerated for up to 1 week.

Makes 15-20 balls

Kasey, Sandy & Drew

Paleo Pumpkin Pie

1 (15 ounce) canned Pumpkin Puree
(or 1½ cup homemade pumpkin puree)
3 Eggs
½ cup Coconut Milk
½ cup Honey
1 tbsp ground Cinnamon
1 tsp Nutmeg
1/8 tsp Celtic Sea Salt
1 Paleo Pie Crust, unbaked

In a food processor combine pumpkin puree, and eggs.
Pulse in coconut milk, honey, cinnamon, nutmeg, and salt
Pour filling into Paleo Pie Crust. Bake at 350° for 45 minutes
Allow to cool then refrigerate for 2 hours to set up

Wilma & Mark
2014

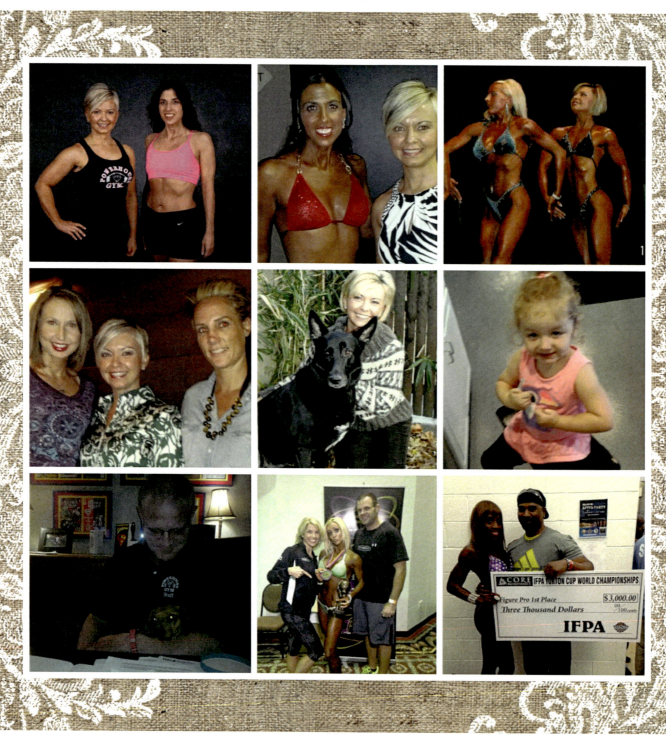

Integrity Training

> DON'T TRY AND BE SOMEONE ELSE'S IDEA OF HEALTHY, FIT OR FEMININE.
>
> YOU HAVE THE MOST AMAZING OPPORTUNITY TO BE EXACTLY WHO YOU ARE! AND THERE AIN'T NO ONE ELSE LIKE YOU.
>
> ロロロ

Dedications

"My sincerest gratitude to Roger Semsch. You helped make me what I am today. Without your belief in me and the doors you opened to allow me to grow, many people would not have the health and wellness they do. For that I am eternally grateful to you and to Powerhouse Gym."

Poncho

Jolie

Jed

Gray Kitty

Meko

Molly

Cannon and Jolie

Dedications

This is my assistant, if you haven't met her. Thank you Natasha for all that you do for me, Molly and Integrity. You make my life possible. We love you very much. Thank you:)

This book is dedicated to my amazing staff of Integrity trainers and clients. You are my family and my reason for jumping out of bed to do what I do. Thank you for participating in this book. I thank God for the opportunity to work with each of you.

I can do all things through Christ who strengthens me.
Phillipines 4:13

Debbie & Natasha
2014

Molly
2014

"I can do all things through Christ who strengthens me."
—Philippians 4:13

INTEGRITY TRAINING ✝ SYSTEMS

Debbie Portell
636.299.2208
[e]: debbiecooperportell@yahoo.com
www.integritytraininggroup.com
www.debbieportell.com

Made in the USA
Middletown, DE
12 January 2015